Dear Jane

Hope you enjoy this libretto. Love, Mother

Typeset by York House Typographic Limited.
Originated, printed and bound by Sagdos in Italy.

ISBN 0 671-65294 X

Carmen

an opera in four acts
by
Georges Bizet

Libretto by
Henri Meilhac
and
Ludovic Halévy

Pagoda Books
Simon & Schuster

Carmen

an opera in four acts
by
Georges Bizet

◄•►

fully illustrated
by
Wendy Corbett

◄•►

introduced
by
José Carreras

◄•►

Royal
Opera
Covent Garden
House

FOREWORD

There is no doubt that *Carmen* is one of the greatest operas ever written, and Don José is one of the parts I most enjoy performing. I first sang the role in 1982, and by February 1987 I will have appeared in the opera for the 100th time. I have been lucky enough to sing the role in the world's leading opera houses, working with many distinguished colleagues.

In the course of the opera, we see Don José first of all as a naive and unsophisticated man; he discovers love for the first time with Carmen but then he ends by destroying himself. He is a loser, a violent personality who is unable to rise above circumstances. He does not know how to fight against fate.

Don José's character is revealed to the audience not only through Bizet's wonderful music, but also by the words of the opera. The text is a vital part of any musical drama, but especially in a work of the later Romantic period, like *Carmen*. I hope this illustrated libretto will help to introduce this great opera to many people and give them a greater understanding of its extraordinary psychological insight.

José Carreras

INTRODUCTION

One of the most popular of all operas today, whenever and wherever *Carmen* is performed, audiences flock to see it. There have been numerous recordings, and several films, too, of this hardy perennial favourite. It may well come as a surprise, therefore, to learn that the work was actually far from a success at first, created as it was amid tremendous disputes.

Georges Bizet had composed several operas without attaining true recognition by the time he was commissioned in 1873 by the Opéra Comique in Paris to write a new work. Collaborating with the playwright Henri Meilhac and Ludovic Halévy, both also regular librettists for the operettas of Jacques Offenbach, he suggested the subject of *Carmen* to them. His source was a short novel by Prosper Mérimée, concerning a Spanish soldier who fell passionately in love with a gypsy woman, and deserted from his regiment to follow a life of crime: but because the gypsy, Carmen, would not be faithful to him, he killed her, and tells his story to the novel's narrator as he waits for his execution for Carmen's murder.

The nineteenth century Opéra Comique was very much a family theatre, where every opera staged was expected to have a happy ending. Small wonder, then, that the prospect of staging a story such as *Carmen* caused great outrage. During this fraught period of composition, Bizet fought hard with his librettists, who felt bound to tone down the horrors of Mérimée's story. A director of the theatre even resigned because of the nature of the new opera; and the whole rehearsal period was punctuated with strong disagreements and stormy scenes.

Response was initially warm at the first performance on 3rd March 1875, but became much less so as the evening went on. The newspaper critics, too, were hostile, and as a result audiences were poor for subsequent performances. During one of these, Celestiné Galli-Marié, who was playing Carmen, became extremely disturbed during the card scene in Act III. As soon as she came off stage, she fainted; and although able to complete the performance, remained convinced that something terrible had happened, almost as if she had seen tragedy in the cards. Later, news came that Bizet had died that very night.

Although it was some time before *Carmen* became generally popular in France, a staging in Vienna later in 1875 was in fact a great success. For this production, Ernest Guiraud composed recitatives to replace the spoken dialogue of the original version, and it was in this later form that the opera first became widely known. Most recent productions, however, have reverted to the use of spoken dialogue to link Bizet's musical numbers: and in the text on the pages that follow, spoken dialogue has been included, with a number of small cuts, in line with usual theatre practice.

Whatever the arguments between Bizet and his librettists, the end result is what today is regarded as a masterly operatic work; and although some of the violence which is explicit in Mérimée's portrait of José was softened, it remains a wonderful psychological portrait of a misfit, a weak man who cannot control his passions. Indeed, it is important to remember that José is an outsider, a Basque who does not fit in among the Andalucians of Seville.

The personality of Bizet's heroine, meanwhile, contains much of the wildness originally created by Mérimée: a woman so devoted to freedom that she is prepared to embrace death itself in order not to be possessed. The characters of Micaela and Escamillo, however, were invented by the librettists, and are not to be found in Mérimée's story. Although Micaela might seem to be no more than the typically sweet heroine expected by the Opéra Comique audience, she also provides a necessary reminder of the life that José would like to live but has not the strength of character to choose. Escamillo has much vitality, but fundamentally his role in the work is to emphasize not that Carmen prefers him to José but to show that she maintains her right to choose.

This fully illustrated 'armchair' version reflects much of the colour and vigour of an actual performance, while helping to clarify the story line and emphasizing characterisation. In a letter written in 1875, the Russian composer Pyotr Illyich Tchaikovsky maintained: '*Carmen* is a masterpiece in every sense of the word . . . I am convinced that in ten years, *Carmen* will be the most popular opera in the whole world.' History has proved him right.

John McMurray

The Characters

 Morales,
a corporal

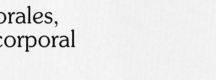 Zuniga,
a lieutenant

Andres,
another lieutenant

 Mercedes,
a friend of Carmen

 Lillas Pastia,
the inn-keeper

Dancairo,
a smuggler

 Micaëla,
a young girl

 Don José,
a corporal

 Carmen,
a gipsy

 Frasquita,
a friend of Carmen

 Escamillo,
a toreador

 Remendado,
another smuggler

Act One

In which the lone-wolf soldier, Don José, first tangles with the dazzling gipsy, Carmen – a fateful hour in both young lives under the scorching sun of Seville.

Here's a young girl who seems to want to talk to us. Look! She's turning this way, she's stopping...

Let's see if we can help!

What are you looking for, my lovely?

I'm looking for a corporal.

Here I am — right here!

The one I want's called José. Do you know him?

José? We all know him.

You do? Is he here with you?

He's not the corporal in our platoon.

He'll be here with the guard that's replacing us when we go off duty.

So he's not here?

No, my lovely, he's not here, but he will be soon. He'll be with the guard that's due to replace us, when we go off duty.

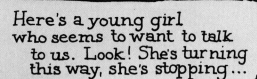

Bugles sound, and crowds gather to watch the changing of the dragoon guard.

The new guard enters; and following close behind, a group of young urchins mimics their marching and tries to keep pace.

Bugles continue to sound, meanwhile.

When the new guard
                comes on duty,
You will see us marching, too!
And you'll hear
            the trumpet sounding,
Ta-ra-ta-ta, ta-ra-ta-ta!

Our heads held proudly,
Just like little soldiers, do.
Left, right, left –
            we're in step, too:
Ta-ra-ta-ta, ta-ra-ta-ta!

Shoulders back.
Chests out to match,
Our arms by our sides.
When the new guard
            comes on duty,
You will see us marching, too!

And you'll hear
the trumpet sounding.
Ta-ra-ta-ta,
        ta-ra-ta-ta!

Squad, right wheel! Squad, halt! Squad, present arms!

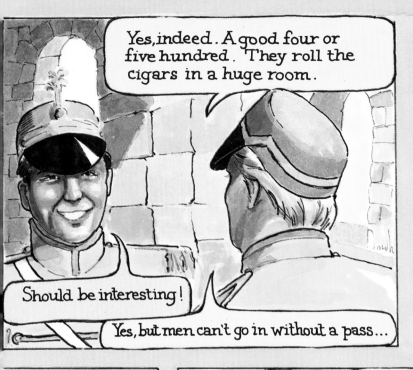

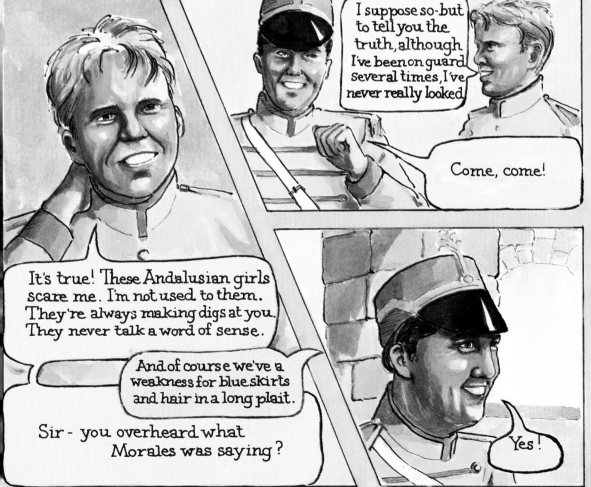

You're a Basque?

And from an old Christian family. My name is Don José Lizzarebengoa. I was intended for the priesthood and started to study for it. But it was a waste of time. I was too fond of playing pelota. One day, after I had just won a game, a boy from the Alava picked a quarrel with me. I got the better of him, but I had to leave the country.

I enlisted in the army! My father was no longer alive, so my mother followed me and came to live twenty miles outside Seville... with young Micaela, an orphan she'd adopted and who didn't want to leave her...

And how old is young Micaela?

Seventeen...

You should have told me that right away. I understand now why you can't tell me whether the factory girls are pretty or not.

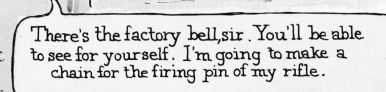

There's the factory bell, sir. You'll be able to see for yourself. I'm going to make a chain for the firing pin of my rifle.

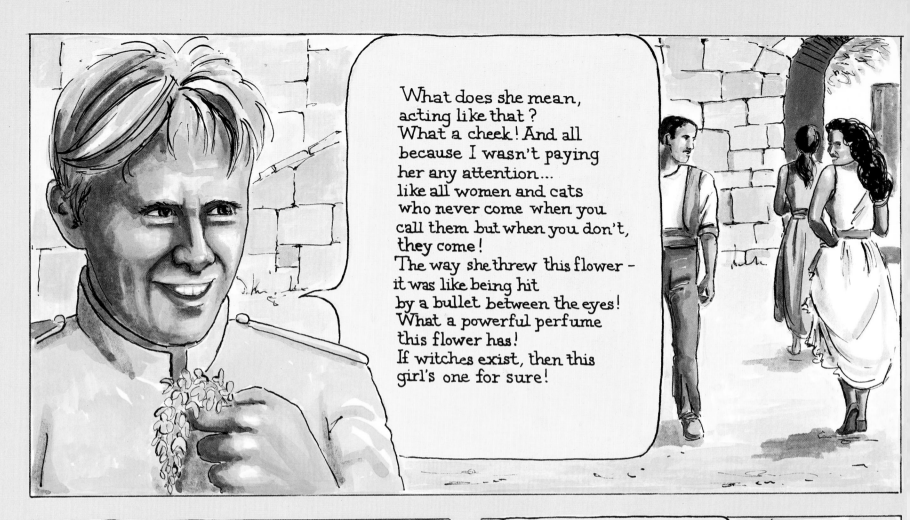

25

Yes, I'll tell you, and I'll give you what she gave me for you. We were coming out of church together when your mother kissed me and said: go to Seville and look for my son, José. It won't take you long.

Tell him that his mother thinks about him night and day, that she's sorry for him, and wants to forgive him for what he's done, and long's to see him again.

Tell him all that, my dear, and give him a kiss from me.

A kiss from my mother?

A kiss for her son! José—here it is, just as I promised her.

And to think I might have been led astray by some devil! My mother's looking after me, as far away as she is. The kiss she's sent me will keep her child safe from harm!

I can see her now... the village, too! So many memories of the past and of my home... You give me new hope and strength. What wonderful memories! Yes, I can see her now... and the village where I lived.

He can see her now, the village, too! So many memories of the past and of his home. They give him new hope and strength. What wonderful memories! Yes, he can see her now... and the village where he lived.

What devil? What harm? I don't understand what you're saying...

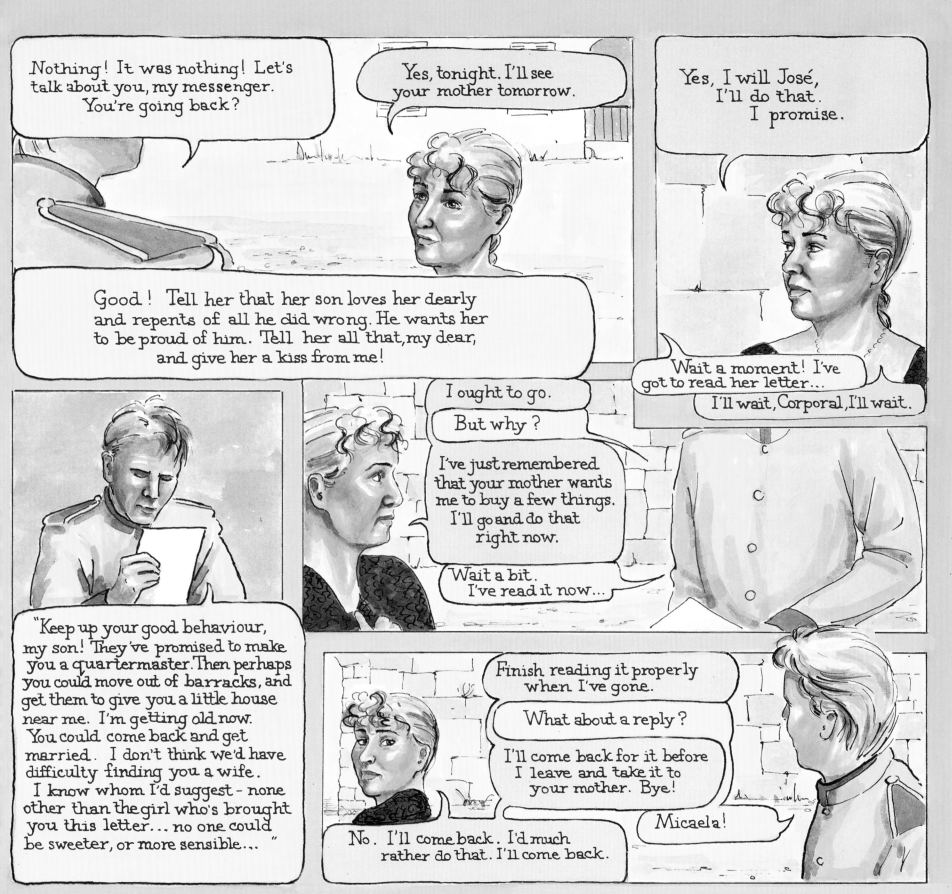

29

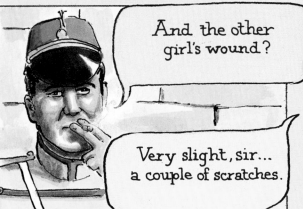

33

Very well, officer, just as you please.
You've forbidden me to speak:
I won't say another word...

By the old walls of Sevilla
Down at my friend's,
Lillas Pastia's,
I'll go and dance the Sequidilla,
And I'll drink manzanilla.
I'll visit my friend,
Lillas Pastia!
Yes, but it's boring on one's own,
And couples really have more fun...
So, just to keep me company,
I'll take the man that I've just won!
        That I've just won?
        ...What am I saying?

I finished with him yesterday.
Now my poor heart
is for-the-taking,
And it's free to go its way...
Though men come flocking
by the dozen,
None of them measures
up to much,
And with the week's end
coming nearer,
Who will love me?
I would love him.
        Who wants my heart?
        It can be taken...

You stand in the nick
of time!
I won't wait a
moment longer!
Then with my latest
love I'll go...

Be quiet! I told you not to speak to me.

I'm not speaking to you... I'm singing to myself. And I'm thinking – it's not forbidden to think!
I'm thinking about an officer...
an officer who's in love with me...and with whom I could well fall in love, too...

Carmen!

My officer is no captain – not even a lieutenant. He's a mere corporal. That's good enough for a gypsy. I think I'll make do with him!

Carmen, I feel intoxicated! Will you do what you promised if I give in to you? If I fall in love with you, would you love me?
We'll go to Lillas Pastia's, just as you said...
Carmen...is that a promise?

Yes, and we can dance the Sequidilla,
And drink manzanilla...
By the old walls of Sevilla,
There's an old inn called Lillas Pastia's.
We'll go and dance the Sequidilla,
And we'll taste his manzanilla.
Tra, la, la, la, la, la, la, la, la, la, la, la.

Watch out! It's the lieutenant!

37

Her hands were tied only loosely; and so, amid the confusion in the crowd, Carmen manages to escape.

Act Two

In which Carmen dances for Don
José in Lillas Pastia's tavern; and fate
conspires with passion, bringing
bloody consequences.

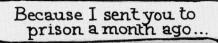

Torero! Would you care to join us? Like you, we all prize skill and courage.

He's coming up!

Gentlemen, I've already told you....

Be so kind as to leave us in peace, Lillas Pastia! And bring us something to drink!

Long live the torero! Long live Escamillo!

On behalf of these ladies and our officers, may I thank you for accepting our invitation.
We didn't want to let you go by without a toast to the great art of bullfighting.

My thanks to you! I can drink a toast to you, too, gentlemen, because soldiers and bullfighters understand each other.

We both take pleasure in fighting.

47

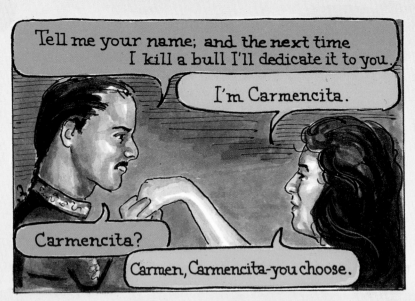

Let me have a go now...

Diamond! Spade! Death!
I was right... and I'm the first.

Then him...
death for
both of us!

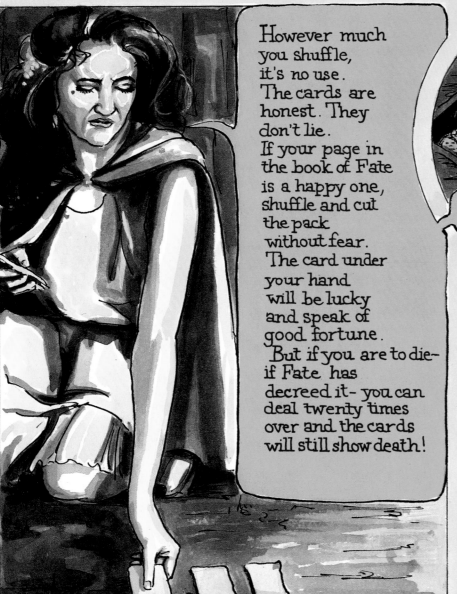

However much
you shuffle,
it's no use.
The cards are
honest. They
don't lie.
If your page in
the book of Fate
is a happy one,
shuffle and cut
the pack
without fear.
The card under
your hand
will be lucky
and speak of
good fortune.
  But if you are to die—
if Fate has
decreed it— you can
deal twenty times
over and the cards
will still show death!

It's death again!

Once more! Tell us
about the future,
fine cards!
Tell all!
Tell us who'll
betray us
and who will
love us!
Speak to us again!

Again and again. There's no
escape. Death. Always death.

Leave the customs men to us.
Like all men, they like being gallant.
We'll go on ahead

We'll deal with the customs men. We'll go on ahead.

They'll be flirtatious!

They'll be charming!

They'll even carry the goods for us!

No... there won't be a problem...
it'll just be a matter of an arm round the waist and some compliments.

And if we have to smile, we'll smile!

And we predict that the contraband will get through.

Come on! We'll go on ahead!
Leave the customs men to us.

We're here.

This is it.

Horrible place isn't it? Doesn't exactly look hospitable.

There's no one around.

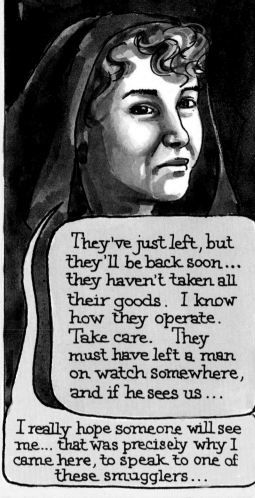

They've just left, but they'll be back soon... they haven't taken all their goods. I know how they operate. Take care. They must have left a man on watch somewhere, and if he sees us...

I really hope someone will see me... that was precisely why I came here, to speak to one of these smugglers...

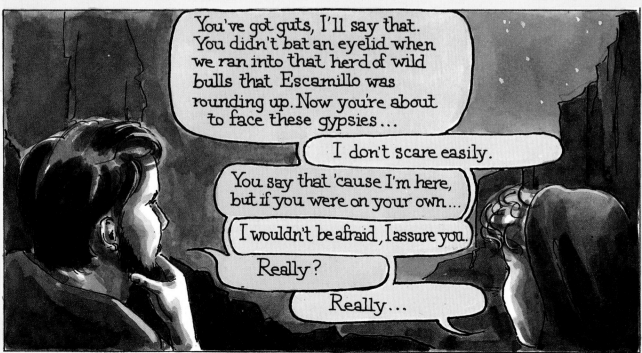

You've got guts, I'll say that. You didn't bat an eyelid when we ran into that herd of wild bulls that Escamillo was rounding up. Now you're about to face these gypsies...

I don't scare easily.

You say that 'cause I'm here, but if you were on your own...

I wouldn't be afraid, I assure you.

Really?

Really...

Can I go then? I agreed to be your guide because you paid me well: but now you're here, I'd prefer to wait where we met - at the inn at the foot of the mountain.

Fine ; wait for me there.

You're going to stay ?

Yes. I'm staying.

May all the saints protect you! What you're doing is quite crazy...

My guide was right. It's not a hospitable place...
I said nothing scared me, that I could fend for myself.
But it's no use trying to act bravely when deep down
I'm dying of fright... I'm afraid, alone in this wild place.
But I'm wrong to be afraid because you, Lord,
will give me courage and protect me.
I shall get a good look at the woman
whose wicked tricks have led astray the man
I really love!
She's dangerous, and she's beautiful. But I don't want
to show I'm afraid! I'll speak up when I meet her.
You'll keep me safe, Lord!

But... no, I'm not wrong – there's José on that rock just a hundred yards away –

José! José!

What's he up to? He's not looking this way.
He's loading his rifle.
He's taking aim. He's going to fire.
Oh my God! I'm not that brave!
I'm scared to death!

A couple of inches lower ... and I wouldn't be in the ring to fight those bulls I've just rounded up...

Who are you? Answer!

Hey! Steady on!

I'm Escamillo, torero from Granada...

Escamillo!

The same!

I know your name. You're welcome here. But truly, my friend, this could have been your last resting place!

That's so. But I'm madly in love, and I'd be a poor sort if I wasn't prepared to risk my life to see my lady.

The one you love is up here?

Just so. She's one of the gypsy girls.

What's her name?

Carmen.

José!

Carmen! To think that it's you who's saved my life!

Escamillo!

As for you, handsome soldier, we're even now. We'll have the decider any time and place you say.

Good! No more fighting now! We must be off!

Goodnight to you.

Before I go, allow me at least to invite you all to the corrida at Seville. I expect to do very well there,

Those who love me will come.

Easy there, my friend!

For now, I bid you farewell.